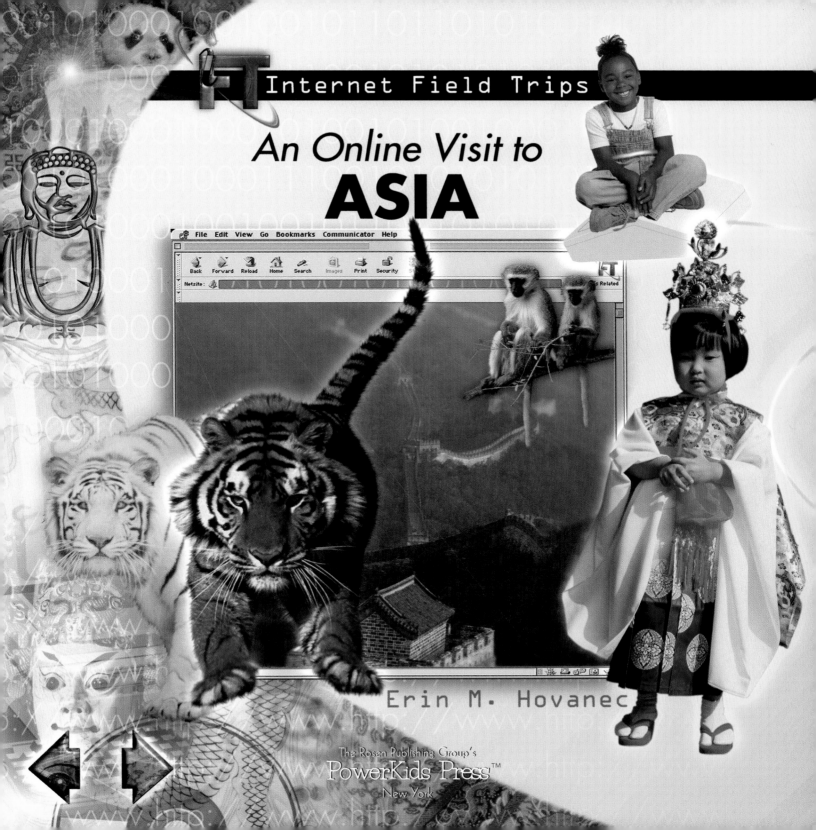

Internet Field Trips

An Online Visit to
ASIA

Erin M. Hovanec

The Rosen Publishing Group's
PowerKids Press™
New York

For my grandfather, Jerry Conway

Published in 2001 by The Rosen Publishing Group, Inc.
29 East 21st Street, New York, NY 10010

First Edition

Book Design: Maria Melendez

Photo Credits: Cover, title page, p.15 (panda, Chinese mask, vase) © SuperStock, cover, title page (Bengal tiger, monkeys) © Digital Stock; cover, title page (Japanese girl, white tiger) © H. Armstrong Roberts, cover, title page, p. 7 (Great Wall of China) © Alison Wright/CORBIS, cover, title page (girl on mouse) © Rubberball Productions; p. 8 (monsoon boat) © Tim Page/CORBIS; p. 11 (Shanghai street) © International Stock; p. 12 (Mount Everest) © International Stock; p. 16 (Japanese girls) © H. Armstrong Roberts; p. 19 (rice paddy) © International Stock; p. 20 (Taj Mahal) © International Stock.

Hovanec, Erin M.
      An online visit to Asia / Erin Hovanec.—1st ed.
        p. cm.— (Internet field trips)
      Includes index.
      ISBN 0-8239-5652-0 (alk. paper)
      1. Asia—Computer network resources—Juvenile literature. 2. Asia—Computer network resources—Directories—Juvenile literature.
   3. Web sites—Directories—Juvenile literature. [1. Asia.] I. Title.

   DS5 .H68 2000
   025.0695—dc21   00-035250

Manufactured in the United States of America

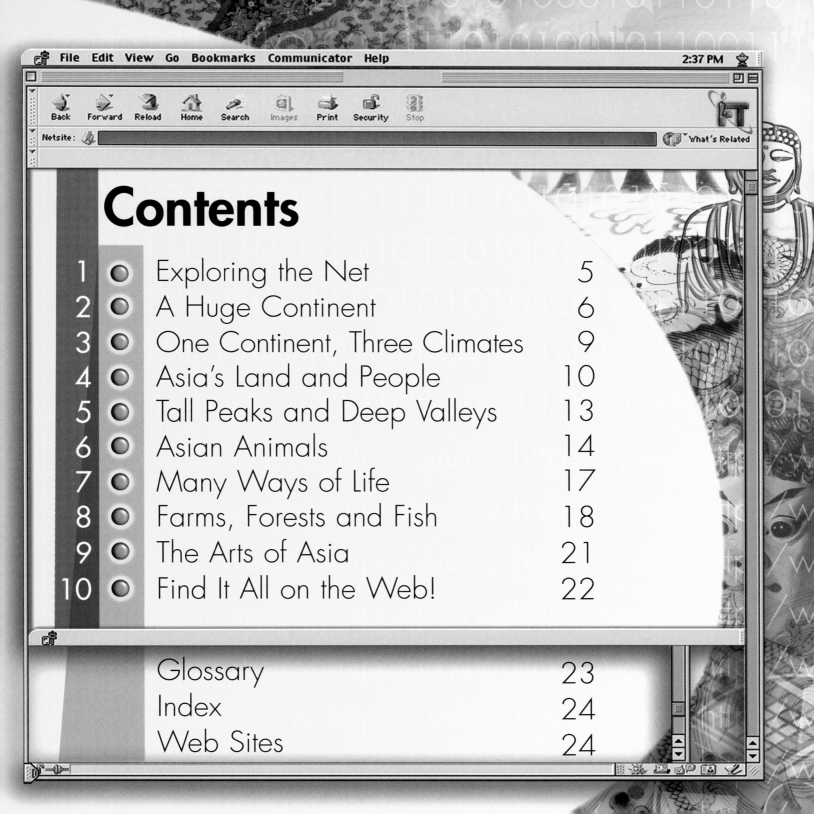

Contents

Getting Connected

To get onto the Internet, you'll need a personal computer. If you don't have one at home, many schools and public libraries make them available to students.

A personal computer

The computer that you use should have a screen, mouse, and keyboard.

A modem

A modem will connect the computer to a telephone line, which connects your computer to computers around the world.

A telephone connection

A telephone connection enables your computer to talk to other computers through a telephone line.

Internet software

Special Internet software makes sure that your computer knows how to use the Internet.

An Internet Service Provider

An Internet service provider is a company that allows you to get on the Internet by charging a small fee every month or year.

Exploring the Net

Imagine what it would be like to take a trip to Asia. The world's biggest continent is filled with interesting people, animals, and natural features. You can travel to Asia on the Internet. The Internet is also called the "Net" or the "Web." It is a network of computers that can help you find information. A computer program called a search engine can help you search the Web. Are you interested in Asia's giant pandas? Type in the words "giant pandas" and the search engine will show a list of hyperlinks. A hyperlink is a colored word that connects one Web page with information about a subject to another page about that same subject.

Here are the supplies that you will need to travel by Internet.

 5

A Huge Continent

Asia is enormous! It is about 17.4 million square miles (45 million sq km) in size. Almost one-third of all the land on Earth is in Asia. The continents of Africa and Europe lie west of Asia. The Pacific Ocean lies to the east of Asia. Countries in northern Asia reach all the way into the freezing Arctic. Countries in southern Asia extend deep into the hot, damp **tropics**.

Asia is not only large in size, it also has the world's largest **population**. Three-fifths of all people on Earth live in Asia. That's a lot of people! If you want to learn more, click to Asia Geographia at http://www.geographia.com/indx04.htm.

6

This globe shows the continent of Asia, where you can find the Great Wall of China.

To learn more about Asia: http://www.lib.utexas.edu/Libs/PCL/Map_collection/asia.html
http://www.askasia.org

To learn more about Asia's climate and weather:
http://www.ems.psu.edu/WeatherWorld
http://www.weather.com

One Continent,
THREE CLIMATES

Although it is only one continent, Asia actually has three types of **climate**. East, South, and parts of Southeast Asia experience **monsoons**. Monsoons are storms with very high winds and heavy rain. More than 300 to 500 inches (762 to 1,270 cm) of rain can fall during some monsoons and cause floods. Central Asia and Mongolia have a very dry climate. The Gobi desert is spread through parts of Mongolia and China. At 500,000 square miles (1.3 million sq km), it is the world's second largest desert. Northern Asia and Asian Russia have very cold climates. Some places in these regions, like Northern Siberia, are frozen year-round.

These fishermen are on the Mekong River in Vietnam during a monsoon.

 9

Asia's Land and People

Asia is so large that it includes South Asia, Southwest Asia, Southeast Asia, East Asia, and Central and North Asia. The 49 countries in this huge continent include Israel, Saudi Arabia, India, Indonesia, and Japan. Asia has some of the world's largest and smallest countries. Russia, the largest country in size on Earth, lies mostly in Asia. It covers more than six and one half million square miles (16.8 million sq km). In contrast, Singapore is very small. This country is 250 square miles (648 km) in size. The People's Republic of China, in East Asia, has the world's largest population. Over one billion people live there.

10

This is a busy street in Shanghai, China. ▶

To learn more about Asia's geography:
http://www.nationalgeographic.com/xpeditions/main.html
http://www.maps.com/atlas/Asia.html

To learn more about Asia's natural wonders:
http://www.thetech.org/exhibits_events/online/everest
http://parks.yahoo.com/parks/international/asia

Tall Peaks
and DEEP VALLEYS

Asia has tall mountains and deep valleys. It has wide seas and winding rivers. It also has dry deserts and wet rain forests. Asia has more mountains than any other continent! One long mountain range extends from India in the south to Tajikistan in the north. The highest point on Earth, Mount Everest, lies between the countries of Nepal and Tibet. Mount Everest peaks at 29,028 feet (8,848 m). This towering mountain is called the "roof of the world." Earth's lowest point can be found in the countries of Israel and Jordan on the shores of the Dead Sea. Parts of the Dead Sea lie 1,300 feet (396.2 m) below **sea level**.

Mount Everest, the highest mountain in the world, lies in the countries of Tibet and Nepal.

13

Asian Animals

Animals such as bears, otters, lynxes, and wolves live in northern Asia. In Tibet yaks provide milk and carry heavy loads. The yak is a long-haired ox. In southern Asia, you'll find monkeys everywhere, along with flying squirrels, crocodiles, snakes, and lizards. Unfortunately, some of Asia's animals are in danger of becoming **extinct**. Asia's large population makes it hard for many animals to find food and shelter. People are building cities in areas where animals have lived for thousands of years. Two species in danger of becoming extinct are the Asian elephant and the giant panda.

14

Giant pandas, like this baby giant panda, are in danger of becoming extinct. ▶

To learn more about endangered species:
http://www.amnh.org/Exhibition/Endangered
http://www.panda.org/kids/wildlife

To learn more about the peoples and cultures in Asia:
http://www.jinjapan.org/kidsweb
http://www.asianculture.org

Many Ways of Life

The vast continent of Asia has many different **ethnic groups**. The Chinese are Asia's largest ethnic group. The Japanese make up the second largest ethnic group. About 70 percent of Asian people live in rural areas. The rest live in cities. Some parts of Asia are very crowded, while others have very few people. Asian people speak many different languages. One language, Chinese, is the most spoken language in the world! All of the world's major religions began in Asia. Buddhism, Christianity, Confucianism, Hinduism, Islam, Judaism, and Taoism all have Asian roots. People around the world still practice these religions.

◀ *These Japanese girls are dressed in the traditional clothing of Japan.*

  17

Farms, Forests _and_ FISH

What kinds of jobs do people in Asia have? More than half of all the people in Asia work in **agriculture.** Farming and raising **livestock** is Asia's biggest **industry.** Many people grow rice and wheat to feed their families and to sell to other countries. Others raise crops like rubber and tea to sell to people outside of Asia. Forestry is another popular industry. Asia has large forests that produce valuable wood for **timber**. The fishing industry is also very important, especially in Japan and China. Asia has rich natural **resources**, such as petroleum, tin, iron, and gold. These resources are sold around the world.

18

This man is planting rice in a rice paddy. Rice paddies are wet lands where rice is grown. ▶

File   Edit   View   Go   Bookmarks   Communicator   Help   2:37 PM

Back   Forward   Reload   Home   Search   Images   Print   Security   Stop

Netsite: What's Related

To learn more about industry in Asia:
http://www.odci.gov/cia/publications/factbook
http://www.your-nation.com

To learn more about the arts of Asia
http://www.ethnographica.com
http://www.metmuseum.org/collections/department.asp?dep=6

The Arts of Asia

From **architecture**, ceramics, and jewelry, to painting, carpet making, and sculpture, Asia is world-famous for its amazing artwork. Parts of Asia are particularly well-known for certain arts. Southwest Asia is famous for its architecture, particularly for buildings called **mosques**. Central Asia is known for its skillful carpet making. South Asia, especially Indonesia and Malaysia, is famous for its beautiful dances. In these dances, each movement has meaning and tells a story. Japan has many art forms including painting and sculpture. Japanese gardens are another form of art. They are simple, yet beautiful.

◀ *The Taj Mahal in Agra, India, is thought to be one of the most beautiful buildings in the world.*

21

Find It All on the Web!

What else would you like to know about Asia? Whatever your interests are, you can find information on the Internet. From animals to agriculture to art, from maps to monsoons to Mount Everest, it's all on the Net.

Asia is a special and exciting continent filled with many different countries. Life in Asia is always changing. If you want to know up-to-the-minute facts about Asia, the Internet can help you find them. Click to Asia Source at http://www.asiasource.org to find out what's happening in Asia today.

G L O S S A R Y

architecture (AR-kih-TEK-cher) The work of designing and constructing buildings.

agriculture (AH-grih-kuhl-cher) The practice of farming or raising livestock.

climate (KLY-mit) The type of weather that certain areas have.

cultures (KUL-cherz) The beliefs, customs, art, and religions of groups of people.

ethnic groups (ETH-nik GROOPS) Groups of people belonging to the same race, culture, or country.

extinct (ik-STINKT) To no longer exist.

industry (In-dus-tree) A business that makes a product or provides a service.

livestock (LYV-stok) Farm animals.

monsoons (MAHN-soonz) A type of weather that brings high winds and heavy rains.

mosques (MAHSKS) Buildings used for worship.

population (pop-yoo-LAY-shun) The number of people who live in a region.

resources (REE-sors-ez) Supplies or sources of energy or useful materials.

sea level (SEE LEHV-el) A way to measure how high or low something is on Earth's surface.

timber (TIM-bur) Wood that is cut and used for building houses, ships, and other wooden objects.

tropics (TRAH-piks) The warm parts of Earth that are near the equator.

23

Index

A
animals, 14
Arctic, 6
artwork, 21

C
climate, 9

D
Dead Sea, 13
desert, 9, 13

E
ethnic groups, 17

I
industry, 18

L
languages, 17

M
mountains, 13
Mount Everest, 13, 22

P
population, 6, 10, 14

R
religions, 17
resources, 18

T
tropics, 6

Web Sites

There are lots of exciting web sites about Asia: Check them out on the following pages: pp., 6, 7, 8, 11, 12, 15, 16, 19, 20, and 22.